THE EMPTY BEDROOM

**The story of one woman's
loss and spiritual renewal**

GRACE KESHISHYAN

Dear Barbara,
Thank you for the book.

In Gratitude!

Grace Keshishyan

First Edition: 2015

Publisher's Cataloging-in-Publication data:
Keshishyan, Grace.
The empty bedroom / Grace Keshishyan. — 1st ed.
56 p. ; 21 cm.
1. Death—Psychological aspects.
2. Bereavement—Psychological aspects.
3. Spiritual healing.
4. Emotional health. 4. Afterlife.

ISBN-978-0-9967727-0-9

www.theemptybedroom.com

Design by Ishkhan Jinbashian
and Raffi Antounian

First Edition

Printed in the United States of America

To my son,
who touched many hearts.
I will forever love you.

The real trouble with this world of ours is that it is not an unreasonable world, nor even that it is a reasonable one. The commonest kind of trouble is that it is nearly reasonable, but not quite. Life is not an illogicality; yet it is a trap for logicians. It looks just a little more mathematical and regular than it is; its exactitude is obvious, but its inexactitude is hidden; its wildness lies in wait.

Gilbert K. Chesterton

Contents

Acknowledgments 9

Introduction 11

The intuition 15

Chapter one: Just be 17

Chapter two: The day of the accident 22

Chapter three: The funeral 25

Chapter four: How my son died 28

Chapter five: Experiences 34

Chapter six: Healing and the future 45

The purpose 47

Thoughts from my heart 50

Poems:

Ephemeral 51

Now I dance 53

Six months 54

Further reading 56

Acknowledgments

The emotional support, unconditional love, friendship, and encouragement I have received from the people in my circle of life have given me the strength to write this book. Thank you all.

I am grateful to Dr. Hanna, whose valuable advice kept me going.

I am grateful to my good friend and colleague Luis Cruz, who listened to me day in and day out, whenever I needed to talk. Your wise words helped me tremendously, Luis.

There is also quite a long list of friends and peers, including Ron Rivera, Miguel Acuna, Laila Honda, George Prokopenko, and Eddie Husain, each of whom helped me without even realizing it. Thank you all for your support at work, which I needed the most to help transform my personal life.

My gratitude goes to my dear friends Seta, Daniel, and Diana, as well as my cousins, who were there in times of sadness and happiness alike. The list is very long and you know who you are.

I am fortunate to have my family. My mom is my role model, the first to cheer me up and the first to cry with me. My sisters Amy and Stephanie; my brother-in-law Robert; my nephews Garik, Khosrov, and Anthony; and my niece Brigitte, you have always been there for me, cheered me up, and supported in any way you could. Thanks a million.

My lovely daughter Marine, I am blessed and grateful to have you in my life. I cannot begin to imagine how I would have survived without you. I am happy to see your family around you. I am grateful to my grandson Henry — your big smile and smart, twinkling eyes bring contentment to my life.

9

Many thanks to Tom Julian for encouraging me, helping me write this book, and suggesting ideas for the title. I'd like to thank Lilit Grigoryan for technical editing; Ishkhan Jinbashian for the general editing and layout of the book; and Paul Hammond for his encouragement and suggestion of ideas with regard to the cover photo. Many thanks to graphic designer Raffi Antounian, who volunteered to help design the book's cover and meticulously fine-tuned the photos.

Finally, I am grateful to you, my reader. I hope you can find some relief in these pages and start your own healing process.

Grace Keshishyan

Introduction

The devastation of losing a child never quite goes away. No matter how many years separate us from the tragedy, the heartache always looms, often returning in waves, to crush and paralyze us once more. Yet at some point in the sustained nightmare of grappling with the sense of pointlessness that accompanies inconsolable grief, something seems to click faintly inside: ever so slowly, and at first with great hesitation, we seem to stumble on a source of strength to embrace another day, and to broaden our horizon in order to find a slightly, perhaps even significantly, recalibrated purpose in the special occasion that's life. This improbable breakthrough, this renewed daring to see life as a special gift worth celebrating, despite our ever-painful awareness that it was snatched away from our own child, may well be the key to a process of healing.

I lost my son, Carl, in 2005. He was 19 years old. Sometimes it feels as though it were yesterday. I miss him very much. I remember the day he was born. The memories created over his lifetime play like a film in my head. Now his bedroom, once full of life and laughter, is eerily empty, languishing in utter silence.

The experience of losing a child scars us for life. We never fully recover from the pain. It ebbs and flows. Most days I'm able to handle it "gracefully," by remembering the good times. Then there are those moments when the pain barrels down on me like a violent storm, trapping my heart in a cage. Usually that's when I take a drive to the Pickwick Ice Hockey Center, in Burbank, California, where my son played hockey. I stand in front of the jersey that hangs on the wall in his memory. I get a cup of hot chocolate, just like the old days, and sit on the bench to watch a hockey game.

We know from physics that energy is never lost, irrespective of its relative strength. The universe is constantly expanding, and the energy released by all matter, including human beings, living or deceased, continues to fuel that expansion. We are, literally, stardust — part and parcel of the universe, even after we stop walking the Earth.

When we are born, there is energy in our physical body and it's held down by gravity. When we die, our energy takes another form and travels up, since there is no physical body and no gravitation to hold it down. It dissipates into dimensions unseen by human eyes and unknown to human minds.

Grief forces us to question our values, priorities, and goals. It compels us to reevaluate our lives. After my son's death, I was gripped by confusion and doubt. I began to question my faith and sought solitude, deliberately disconnecting myself from the world.

Following my son's funeral, I was furious at God. Far from willing to pray, I asked him, "Why? Why have you done this to him — and to me? How can I pray now? I had faith in you, and the only thing I have asked was to keep my son out of harm's way. You couldn't do that."

I had locked myself in complete despair. I thought there was no way out.

Yet what I could not possibly fathom in that depth of despair was the fact that the human spirit is malleable to an inconceivable degree, with a built-in survival mechanism which can not only help us cope with adversity, but enable us to perceive a given situation through a fresh lens, in effect empowering us to transform our reality.

It took time. And it took seemingly interminable stretches of reflection. As I struggled to find answers as to why my son was taken away from me, I slowly but surely began to emerge from the darkness. The breakthrough, almost a Eureka moment, came in the form of the realization that in fact my hand had always been held by a universal power — that which we might call God; that which I knew to be God.

God is everywhere. He is the universe. He is in the mountains I hike, the air I breathe, the people I say hello and goodbye to. He is in the things I don't see with my own eyes, in dimensions that the human mind cannot comprehend yet. He is the energy, love, and life force behind everything... from sunrise to sunset.

The process of perceiving the world anew also had unexpected concomitants. In my dreams, my son showed me where he was affording me glimpses of what we might refer to as the afterlife. I know he is no longer in the material world, but I'm also certain that he is in a dimension we know nothing about. I am convinced of this because I was there with him. As significantly, there have been numerous instances where I have felt my son's presence in a form of energy that surrounds me. It has felt as though he was hugging me with his energy. I acknowledge and accept these experiences, given their indisputable realness, their palpability. I know they are my son's way of communicating and saying, "Here I am, mom, still around... giving you a sign that there is an afterlife and it is wonderful!"

The intuition

I knew immediately something was terribly wrong, but you can know that and not allow the thought in your head, at the front of your head. It dances around at the back, where it can't be controlled. But the front of the head is where the pain begins.

Sebastian Barry,
The Secret Scripture

December 6, 2005

Eleven days before going on vacation with a group of friends to Big Bear, a mountain resort in California, my son celebrated his birthday with a big party. At one point during the evening, he suddenly looked at his buddies and told them he had a very strange feeling that something was going to happen to him. He couldn't explain what it was, but felt it very strongly and couldn't figure out why he felt the way he did.

His friends gave him a puzzled look and said he was talking nonsense. My son innocently replied that he hoped it meant nothing.

Eleven days later, he was gone.

Chapter one

Just be

Grief fills the room up of my absent child,
Lies in his bed, walks up and down with me,
Puts on his pretty look, repeats his words,
Remembers me of his gracious parts,
Stuffs out his vacant garments with his form.
William Shakespeare

I would like to sit with you today and have a conversation about the loss of your child to an accidental or other type of untimely death.

When it comes so unexpectedly, so suddenly, death does not quietly make the light fade out, nor does it warn you of the ensuing pain. It just strikes so hard and so quickly that there is no explaining the impact. I know quite well the shock and hollowness you feel within, how immediate the darkness is. Yet I also know that it is possible to see the light of healing after such a catastrophic loss.

I don't say this lightly. I say it with utmost respect for your grief, as I have experienced the loss of my own son, Carl, at the tender age of 19.

I wrote this book to share with you the personal devastation and eventual awakenings I have experienced, in hopes of helping you cope with your own grief.

I have read many books, struggled with a ton of questions, and had numerous talks with people who have experienced a similar loss. To hear about what they have gone through has helped me tremendously.

I know only too well that your pain feels unbearable, and there is no one who can console your broken heart, which has left you feeling empty-handed. That pain also has the power to make you fall to your knees more times than not, and it is never easy. Grief is unique to each person: some feel numb, some feel irritable and restless, some often break into tears, and many withdraw into themselves. You might also find yourself being overcome by feelings you never knew could develop in you.

These roller-coaster emotions somehow help us alleviate a small measure of our pain while time will help us endure what must be endured. In my own experience, staying in that special moment that we receive each morning called today has been a key strategy. I no longer think about tomorrow. Tomorrow will take care of itself.

At the initial stage of your grief, however, when that place of inner peace is simply out of reach, you are dealing with a wound so tender that as yet you cannot do anything to heal it. What was customary for you to do before now seems a gargantuan task. You find solace in absolutely nothing except letting everything go. What was uncomfortable becomes comfortable. In fact, if you are not careful, you can lose your own life while you are grieving the death of a loved one. You might feel that life itself is foolish and meaningless, to the point that thinking clearly stops being an option.

The purpose of this book is to help you become aware of the vital importance of expressing your grief. You must find your own way of doing this, whether it be through reading, writing, painting, music, exercise, or talking to people who have gone through a similar experience — you'd be surprised to hear what others have gone through.

As you begin the initially difficult process of expressing your grief, and address each emotion and thought within the context of willing to share them with others, you will benefit enormously from the support given you by family, friends, people with similar experiences, and, if available, church groups or other support networks. Books about dealing with the sorrow of the untimely death of a loved one can also be wonderful sources of help.

I will have some specific suggestions for you in my concluding chapter.

The healing will start within the wound. I know this probably doesn't make sense to you now, but it will. For now, I hope you will learn to simply... be.

What do you do?

Sometimes you might feel there must be something that can be done, somewhere to go, someone to talk to, a conference to attend. You feel guilt, sadness, depression, anger, and the need to be normal again, all at the same time. You just think that your life has been transformed into something you can't put your finger on, something spinning terrifyingly out of control.

This is exactly where you have to just be.

Nurturing the emotions welling up inside you is very important. Learn to be tearful. Tears are a gift that help us release all that has bottled up inside. Relief is at hand.

I do realize that we have responsibilities to attend to. We need to function "normally" in order to work, drive, shop, communicate with others, and keep the household running, because these are all integral parts of our lives. So sometimes we must control our emotions of grief and learn to be: to be in the moment of carrying out our responsibilities, even if others may not understand what is happening inside us.

Do things that give you some much needed, albeit temporary, relief. Share your feeling with people you trust and care for. If you withdraw into your cocoon and continue to numb yourself in any way you can, you will delay the healing process and make it even more difficult.

It is important to note that tears are not a sign of weakness. They're certainly not gender-specific. There's a stigma out there regarding men who break into tears, driven by a still-common perception that men need to be tough and not display their emotions. This couldn't be further from the truth. To my male readers I say emphatically, Please do not hide behind some bloated notion of masculinity, thinking that it is wrong to cry, that even though you have suffered a loss, your responsibility is to act as though it can't possibly get to you. You are a human being and the loss of a loved one, a child in particular, affects everyone.

I had to learn that each person deals with grief differently. Some who know you and are familiar with your pain don't know what to say when they see you. Others say things to comfort you, but sometimes may unwittingly end up making you sadder still.

Lastly you must consider the importance of your family.

If you have other children, do everything you can not to neglect them. I know it is easy to do so. As parents, we love our children unconditionally and don't want anything bad to happen to any of them. When we're grieving, we temporary become incapable of thinking clearly, or acting properly, consequently even failing to notice our family. Yet our spouses, children, and other family members are still alive, and, as hard as it may seem to believe and understand, they are also in pain and grieving as much as you are. I remember when my daughter came to me and said, "Mom, I'm here for you but I am in pain too. I'm here, alive, and need your help."

That's when I realized I still had to live and take on my responsibilities, to be there for my other child, regardless of what seemingly insurmountable challenges had been placed before me. In such situations, families can either heal and ultimately become a stronger unit, or can break apart and no longer be connected.

Yes, compel yourself into the habit of just being. Be open to having discussions with your children and spouse, and those family members who are also hurting. There may be ten or more different hearts within your family and its immediate circle that are grieving and confused as to how to handle their pain, and whose lives are in disarray because of it.

It's perfectly okay to feel the pain. It's okay to become numb to others. And it's okay to suspect that you're never going to feel normal again. Yet it will do you a world of good to open yourself to the certainty that there is healing waiting to be embraced. I hope my experiences will help you become convinced of that certainty.

Chapter two

The day of the accident

When you reach the end of what you should know, you will be at the beginning of what you should sense.

Kahlil Gibran,
Sand and Foam

December 17, 2005

At 12:15 pm on that hectic Saturday, I was busy with work at the office.

It was about this time that I went outside for a lunch break. It was an extraordinarily beautiful day. At one point, as a light breeze caressed my face, my gaze rested on the line of tall eucalyptus trees which protected the jasmine shrubs.

It was marvelous to be sitting outside and basking in the sunshine in the middle of December while it was freezing on the East Coast. After I enjoyed my salad, I got up and walked back to the office, feeling the warmth of the sun on my back.

All of a sudden, I had an excruciating pain — precisely the type of pain that's reminiscent of the pangs of childbirth. It was the pain I felt when I was about to give birth to my son, Carl, 19 years earlier.

I took a pain killer, but it didn't help. It took several hours for the pain to subside. I finished my shift and went home so tired that I ended up going to bed much earlier than I usually do. I also kept thinking of my son, as the pain I experienced reminded me specifically of the day of his birth. I wanted to call him but decided not to, as he had told me not to call him. "I'll call you if I feel like talking," he had said.

First, a little background. My son and I had not talked

for four years. Divorce is a terrible thing. He had decided to live with his father while my daughter had stayed with me.

The next day, I was up at the break of dawn. I could not sleep, so I went for a short walk around the block to get some fresh air while the neighborhood slept. I started to feel uncomfortable again. It wasn't pain this time, but I felt that something was definitely wrong. I was restless and felt sure I was about to hear of a death — of someone very close. I had never been superstitious, but the premonition I felt that morning was overwhelmingly real.

As I walked along the silent, tree-lined street, the peacefulness and beauty surrounding me made for an absolutely mystical moment, yet I was unable to enjoy any of it. That terrible sense of unease held on to me so tightly that I suddenly turned around and headed back home. As I reached our building, I decided to stop by my mom's apartment. To my surprise, she was up.

We sat in her living room. It was still very quiet as she turned on a small light, casting long shadows over the walls. I made some coffee while reflecting on my children and noting how fast time had gone by.

Then the phone rang.

I picked it up. It was a relative. She said my son was in the hospital. I was gripped by panic. I wanted to know which hospital he was in. My son had been injured while on vacation with friends in Big Bear.

I called his father and other members of his family, but couldn't get a hold of anyone. I walked over to look out the window. It was beautiful outside: sunny, with the birds chirping away. Inside me, however, there was a thunderous black cloud.

The phone rang again.

The friend on the phone asked me to sit down. She had bad news for me. She said my son had had an accident the previous day while kayaking. He had drowned at around 12:35 pm. He was taken to Loma Linda Hospital, where he was revived, but then, at around 3:30 pm, he was pronounced dead.

I was dumbfounded. I started yelling and crying hysterically. "It can't be true!" I kept screaming. "It just can't be true!"

Some time later, I found the strength to call my brother-in-law and asked him to come over to help — which he kindly did and confirmed that it was true, my only son was gone.

It's next to impossible to describe what I felt. I was numb, unable to think. My body felt stiff. From one moment to the next, my neck and back became so sore that it felt as though I were carrying an enormous load.

I couldn't eat or drink. I just cried nonstop and kept thinking it couldn't be true. I hoped it was all a horrid nightmare and soon I would wake up and see my son alive.

But it wasn't.

I fell asleep. When I woke up, my sisters told me I had slept for over 36 hours. They were so worried about me that they were about to call an ambulance. I had no energy and my memory was fading.

The life I had known was just sucked out of me. I wanted to die.

Chapter three

The funeral

Farewell! God knows when we shall meet again.
William Shakespeare

My son's funeral was held on December 22, 2005.

I was in a state of complete shock. I was gripped by disbelief and anger. At times I found it hard to breathe. I was non-functional. When I tried to walk towards my son's casket, my knees went numb. If my brother-in-law were not there, I would have collapsed. I saw my son's lifeless body, quietly lying there, his hands cold, his gorgeous eyes shut. The thought that I was seeing him for the last time devastated me. That shock was to be followed by anxiety and panic attacks for years to come.

It felt as though everything that's beautiful in life had disappeared. I thought there was nothing left for me to do except to search for the answer as to why my son was gone.

After the funeral, my panic attacks grew so intense that I decided to see my doctor. I told her about my son's accidental death, and the fact that my panic attacks were triggered by the sight of his casket. No matter where I was, I told her, constricted spaces made me feel there wasn't enough air to breathe and I thought I would faint. I also told her that often, while driving, I needed to exit a freeway and park in a safe area to calm myself down, in order not to cause an accident. I wanted my doctor to help me in any way she could, because the panic attacks were making it dangerous for me to drive, and it was embarrassing when they flared up unexpectedly at work or in public.

To my surprise, said she would not prescribe any medications to numb the pain and suffering. Instead I would have to go through my crisis without any medications, however long it would take. She suggested to start reading about grief and specifically the loss of a child, and to talk to people I felt comfortable with about my experience and emotional state, without filtering anything. I thanked her and left.

Soon I decided to seek a second opinion. The doctor I saw was an elder gentleman, in his mid-60s. After hearing about my condition, he said, "Young lady, I know exactly what it is you are going through and I am not going to prescribe you anything." Then he said, "Thirty years ago, my 21-year-old son took his own life. Ever since his death, there has not been a day I have not thought of him. This is going to be your new life, where you have to make some adjustments to acknowledge the feelings and emotions you are going through, and take it one day at a time. It has been 30 years and I still have days when I suddenly break into tears. I may be driving down a street where he and I had been once, or a memory comes to mind out of the blue and I miss his physical presence, even though I know his life continues in some other form. There are things that you may discover for yourself and use them to find your way out. But make no mistake: this is going to be part of your new life's journey."

As I left the clinic, at once I realized that despite their different backgrounds, the two doctors had given me more or less the same advice. I drove to the Brand Library Park, where I could walk under the oak and maple trees, to think and connect with the universe around me, to seek some answers from within. I loved that park. I had often hiked the mountains around it. That day, however, I wanted to… just be.

The second doctor's words still rang in my ears: "life continues in some other form," "things that you may discover for yourself and use them to find your way out," "this is going to be part of your new life's journey."

The sunset was beautiful as I was watched it from a window inside Brand Park Library.

Chapter four

How my son died

Some are bound to die young.
By dying young a person stays young
In people's memory.
If he burns brightly before he dies,
His brightness shines for all time.
                                                        Unknown

As any of you who have suffered the loss of a child would know and understand, my trauma persisted long after the funeral. The more I tried to grapple with it, the more it broke me. Yet, somehow, over the course of a few days, I was able to quiet my emotions, just enough to start the process of trying to understand what exactly had happened.

As I knew Carl had been with his friends on that fateful day, I wanted to talk to them in order to reconstruct the events that had led to his death.

I invited his friends over to my house for a quiet conversation, and to get some answers to the many questions that still weighed heavy on my heart. If, as a grieving mother, inviting the young men over to discuss the death of their friend wasn't an easy request to make, I can only imagine how much harder it was for them to receive it. I'm sure they felt somewhat uneasy and hesitant, but thankfully three of them said yes and I was grateful that they did.

I had so many questions that I just didn't know where to start. Eventually I managed to organize my thoughts into five key issues that had been tormenting me and for which I needed to have some answers, as follows.

First, I wanted to know what exactly had happened when my son and his friends rented a cabin on that cold December in 2005.

Second, I wanted to know about the property they were staying at, in the area called Big Bear Boulder Bay Lake.

Third, I wanted to know about the kayak that Carl was using.

Fourth, I wanted to know every detail of his accident.

And fifth, I wanted to know the particulars of the medical attention he received following the accident.

Again, I can only imagine the extreme anxiety those young men must've felt before coming to see me. They arrived on time, and after the greetings and hugs, went on to share their recollections.

They had rented the cabin from a company called Big Bear Cool Cabins. A representative of the company had given the young men the keys to not only the cabin but also the dock, so they could have access to the lake and a kayak. They were told to make themselves at home, feel free to use the kayak, and enjoy their stay.

Sadly, the cabin personnel had neglected to mention to the young men that the kayak was not registered, that there were no life jackets available, and that the temperature of the lake was 39 degrees. On the contrary, the young men were encouraged to go out and enjoy themselves, despite the fact that no safety measures of any kind were in place. So what do young men, who believe they're invincible, do when they're out in the woods and staying in a cabin? The next morning, as they were discussing how they should spend the day ahead, one of them brought up the subject of the kayak and asked if anyone was up to going out into the lake for some fun.

One of the young men was indeed up to having some fun on the lake. It was Carl, my son.

Some of the young men agreed, but others thought it was too cold to be out there. To Carl, however, the weather was nothing to be concerned about. He was a very good hockey player, with a lot of skating experience. He was confident and the first to take a turn on the kayak. He kayaked all the way to the middle of the lake and back.

As he reached the dock, stepped out of the kayak, and tied the rope to the hook that was attached to the planks, his friends videotaped him. I am so thankful for that video, which I've kept as a prized possession.

Just as Carl's friends were videotaping him, they started to get very cold. Since they had no jackets on, they left him and told him they were going to go back to the cabin and get their jackets and would come back to take their turn.

But they turn would never come.

They had no idea that in their absence, Carl had decided to take the kayak out again instead of waiting for them. As he was making his way back to the middle of the lake, the kayak became unstable and suddenly flipped over, with Carl in it.

Two fisherman who were on the other side of the lake saw the kayak turn over and Carl struggle in the freezing water, frantically trying with all his strength to flip the canoe back up.

The fishermen later said it was at that time that Carl turned the kayak over and got in, but something happened and the kayak became unstable again. Carl fell back into the water, the kayak drifting rapidly away, and it was clear that he was not going to be able to catch up with it. He was all by himself, in the middle of a lake that had a temperature of under 40 degrees.

Time was running out.

The fishermen called out to Carl, telling him to take his heavy jacket off so it would not weigh him down. After he did that, Carl started to swim toward the kayak again. But he was unable to reach it. At that point, as he gave up on the canoe, he used all his remaining strength to turn around and head north, swimming toward the rock island that sat in the middle of the lake.

But he didn't make it.

Meanwhile Carl's panic-stricken friends ran around to ask for help. They knew the next-door neighbor had a big boat. They knocked on the door asking for help, but were not able to get any.

The fishermen and Carl's friends called 911, knowing he was not going to be able to make it. The police were dispatched at 12:34 pm. They arrived seven minutes later, at 12:41 pm. The Big Bear Fire Department was on the scene first, with a medical ambulance, but there were no divers to retrieve Carl right away. Tragically, it took almost two hours before divers could be helicoptered in from another city and recover Carl's body. The medical procedures that were subsequently applied came too late. My son was pronounced dead.

A tragedy that could have been prevented

One year later, I acted on an overwhelming desire to learn more about the last moments of my son's life. I drove to Big Bear and rented the same cabin he had stayed in. I even went down to City Hall to talk to officials, but they refused to see me, turning me away with the excuse that no one connected with Carl's accident was in.

For the first time, I felt that elected officials and people in uniform, whom I've respected and honored all my life, were now acting in a cowardly manner and hiding behind their desks.

Next I went to the San Bernardino Coroner's Office and requested to see all the documents and reports related to my son's death. I could not believe the obvious errors that had been made. They screamed carelessness and ignorance, on the part of incompetent people who were appointed to positions they should never have been in.

Here is what I learned:

When they pulled Carl out of the water, his body temperature was 91.5 degrees.

He was taken to Big Bear Valley Community Hospital, arriving at 2:45 pm.

At 2:46 pm, they performed CPR and placed an Oral Gastric Tube incorrectly. Instead of placing it in the stomach through the esophagus, they placed it in his lungs. Suddenly his body temperature started to drop, falling all the way down to 86 degrees!

At 3 pm, they transferred him by helicopter to Loma Linda Hospital Medical Center, where they found out that the tube was incorrectly placed in his lungs. They removed it at once, but the removal led to profuse blood loss, and Carl's temperature started falling quickly. Despite all of the efforts of the staff at Loma Linda, my son was gone.

Right after learning of the horrible incompetence that had led to my son's death, I sought legal help. The lawyers I saw totally agreed with me that negligence and malpractice were involved, but told me there was nothing we could do since the Statute of Limitations allowed only six months for bringing legal action and I was too late.

I am saddened that my government tells me I have a mere 180 days to find the strength and time to seek justice while wrestling with grief and pain, dealing with the funeral and burial, and a million other details. Who has the energy in such a short time? Who would even have that on their mind as they grieve the loss of a child?

Moreover, even if I were able to file a lawsuit, most likely it would drag for years to come. That was the last thing I wanted to add to my suffering, especially given my realization that nothing could bring my son back.

Instead I decided to help make sure that accidents like this are prevented. I contacted the officials at Big Bear City Hall, requesting that diver teams be stationed nearby in order to respond quickly and adequately to similar accidents. All they could say was, "Sorry for your loss, but this was an accident and we are not going to add any diver teams."

Big Bear… Though there is beauty in the trees, there is apathy in the hearts of those who govern, and the darkness that looms over the lake and cabins make it impossible for me to revisit that place.

In a time of tragedy, how frustrating and demoralizing it is to see elected officials focus on policy and budgets instead of caring for the safety and well-being of the people whose votes put them in office. There was no sympathy at all for my son's death.

Chapter five

Experiences

Sorrow makes us all children again — destroys all differences of intellect. The wisest know nothing.
                                                    Ralph Waldo Emerson

During the time of your grief and afterwards, in fact, for the rest of your life, you might experience things that have no logical explanations because the human mind is not capable of understanding them. These experiences nonetheless help us, and teach us that there is life after death. Since physics has shown that energy is never lost, I believe that neither is human energy.

It is this very belief which allows and sometimes forces us to connect with a higher being. I know we do not pay much attention to these things in our daily lives. Rather, they occur to us only when tragedy strikes and our life is changes forever.

This is when we start to focus on a journey: a journey to find the elusive answer, and one which is so hurtful to search for. Yet certain communications reach us at the visceral level, and we know there is an irreducible truth behind them.

These experiences at first feel unnatural because we cannot see them with our eyes or feel them with our hands. They could manifest themselves in the form of a dream or a sudden sensation.

Such experiences, of course, are often labeled lazily as "paranormal," for all intents and purposes imaginary, while Western medicine and psychology are too eager to "diagnose" them as the tell-tale signs of depression at best, hallucination at worst. I myself was skeptical before these experiences entered my life.

For quite some time, I was hesitant to share them with others as I refused to take them seriously. Eventually, however, as they kept recurring, in so many different ways and places, and without any apparent reason, I found myself awakening to their truth and the fact that they are always around us, if only we choose to acknowledge them.

There is a power around us which connects us to everything seen and unseen by the naked eye. This power, or energy, leaves the physical body and travels to different dimensions. While modern science as yet can't prove the existence of these dimensions and no one knows what happens to a person's energy when he or she ceases to live in the form of a human being, physics has demonstrated indisputably that energy, irrespective of its size, is never lost.

When we are able to comprehend the messages a deceased loved one is passing down to us, grasp them on a conscious level, and have the courage to share them with those around us, we start to look at life and the afterlife through a different lens.

Phenomenal things started happening for me two months after my son's death.

First experience

I had a dream in which I was on a bus and a family member was there playing with a friend. The bus stopped and all of the sudden my son appeared. He got on the bus and walked towards me. I started to cry and said, "Oh, the whole funeral was a lie! I am so grateful that you are alive." He came and quietly sat on my lap, placing his right hand over my shoulder. I could feel his fingers on my right arm. I hugged him around his waist, realizing I couldn't reach and hug his full body anymore since he was all grown up.

I felt his weight on my legs and body, and the warmth of his arm around my shoulder travel down my spine. It was comforting and relaxing. I was in a state of pure bliss.

As I kissed his cheek, he looked very sad and concerned. And then he spoke. "Mom, I am very sorry for all of the wrongs I have done you and I want you to know that I am well. Mom, now I want you to start to think about the family." As he said this, he pointed at the family member who was playing on the bus. "I want you to take care of yourself," he continued. "Don't worry about me, I am well."

I couldn't hold myself back and told him that no matter what had happened in our past, I had always loved him. "I know, mom," he said. "I know everything now." And then he got up and vanished.

I woke up and realized it was just a dream, even though it felt so real. As I moved my pillow, I noticed it was soaked. The tears I had shed in my dream were real. I sat up in bed and noticed that all the stiffness that had been in my back was now gone.

I started to think about this and realized that, as strange as it might've seem, the panic, anger, and frustration which I had been carrying ever since Carl's death were no longer there. For the first time in months, I felt at peace.

I closed my eyes as I couldn't wait to replay the whole dream again in my mind, over and over, every detail of it. It was the most comforting thing I had ever experienced. Afterwards I wrote it all down, so that, in case my memory faded in my old age, I would still have access to the dream.

I wasn't sure how I was going to be able to explain this phenomenon. Naturally I wasn't comfortable with the idea of sharing it with anyone, as I knew they would think grief had driven me crazy.

I reflected on the curious fact that my son had spoken to me just by looking at me, and the fact that I had reciprocated. We had communicated and understood each other without speaking. It had been done simply by gazing, touching. Our minds had spoken to one another.

And while I fully realized that it had been only a dream — how else would we have been able to communicate if not in such a beautiful and colorful dream? — I didn't care how we had communicated. The important thing was that I could see him in my dreams.

Another interesting thing about this experience is that I rarely dream. In fact, I have no recollection of any dreams prior to the one with Carl. But now, at this juncture in my life, I remember every single dream connected with my son, with all their intricate details, including words that were spoken or otherwise communicated. In the particular dream that I just described, he was wearing light blue jeans and a white T-shirt; the bus seats were of black leather; it was an older bus; I was wearing a white dress; the family member on the bus had a ponytail and was wearing black tights and a white T-shirt with prints; and the friend with whom she was playing likewise wore black tights and a yellow T-shirt.

With its powerful vividness, the dream enabled me to make a psychological leap: it helped me decide that I shouldn't worry about what others may believe, and pay attention to the experiences that would come my way. I would open myself up and not question the experience at hand. I would accept things as they came, and be at peace without overanalyzing.

Second experience: March 26, 2006

My son visited me again in my dream. But unlike the previous dream, he was frustrated and said, "Mom, you have got to take me out of here. It's wet and I feel cold. Please, I want you to come and take me away."

I opened my eyes only to see, again, that it had been just

a dream. Yet I knew it was real. I started to panic and cried, not knowing what to do. What did it mean? What was my son trying to tell me? At around 8 am, I left the house and drove straight to the cemetery. When I arrived, I couldn't help but notice that his headstone was tilted to one side. It had rained the night before. A puddle of water covered most of the headstone.

After I placed flowers in the vase in front of the gravesite and headed to the cemetery office to request that my son's headstone be repaired, I suddenly noticed a white car parking by the curb, a few feet from where I was standing. I never saw or heard it pull up. It seemed to appear out of nowhere. An elderly gentleman with white hair and a mustache got out of the car and approached me. He asked if he could be of service. I immediately said yes and showed him the headstone. I asked him if he could fix it and he assured me that he could. Only, he said, he would have to prepare a work order with the appropriate office.

I then felt the courage to ask him how he had arrived because I hadn't seen his car pull up. I went on to share with him the fact that I had been experiencing strange things lately. "Sometimes I feel as if I am going crazy," I said. The gentleman smiled and said, "The order will be placed and the work will be done soon."

Within ten days, my son's headstone was fixed.

I saw my son in dream again. "Thank you, mom," he said and disappeared. Just like that.

Strange, I grew comfortable and accustomed to seeing him in my dreams. I was actually looking forward to going to bed and sleeping, in hopes of seeing and communicating with him.

Third experience: May 22, 2006
In this unforgettable dream, I was standing on the

38

driveway of our property, absolutely awestruck by the fact that whereas the sky above the neighborhood was clear, there were dark clouds hovering just over our house. It was astounding.

All of a sudden, my son emerged from the clouds and ran to me. He hugged me and said, "I am done with dad. I am going to come and live with you. I tried to talk to him and explain a lot of things, but he is not listening. I am done. I am going to stay with you." I tried to comfort him while he was in my arms. But in the dream itself, I realized this was just a dream as I knew my son was dead. I told him, yes, he could stay with me all the time, I would love that.

After I woke up, I visited the cemetery and thought, "How is he going to come and stay with me?"

Then, within a short while, I began to experience new things — things which at first I would consider nothing more than coincidences. These experiences occurred randomly and always without any forethought or preconditioning on my part. In other words, they were not, by a long stretch of the imagination, what you might call self-fulfilling prophecies.

The pattern and substance of these experiences led me to the conviction that my son was with me. And when he was, he made me see, hear, feel, and smell his presence. This was his way of communicating with me.

One day, I arrived at the cemetery at around 5:30 pm, as the sun was setting. The towering pine tree near my son's plot had scattered needles all over the ground. A couple of squirrels were running up and down the tree. As I approached it, the squirrels quickly jumped over to a nearby oak tree.

I put the flowers down and picked up the vase to fill it with water from the fountain, which was about 25 feet away. As I was walking back to his plot, I smelled a waft of cologne traveling with me at nose level. I looked around to see if there was a man around, but I couldn't see anyone. I looked at the other plots, to see if the scent was coming from flowers. The cemetery usually clears flowers from the plots every Wednesday, so there was none to be seen anywhere.

I turned my head and the scent turned with me. It was a distinctly familiar smell yet I couldn't identify it.

When I arrived at Carl's plot, the scent disappeared. I was shocked. I stayed at the cemetery till sunset. It felt wonderful to sit next to his hillside grave and watch the sunset, allowing the memories to play in my head like a film. Though I couldn't see my son, I know he saw me.

The breeze, which softly caressed my face, brought back that fragrance. It also dried the tears gliding down the sides of my cheeks.

After watching the sunset, I got up and drove to the mall to see if I could find the cologne I had smelled at the gravesite. I walked in a crowded mall, by countertops full of cologne and perfume, trying as hard as I could to find that one distinctive scent. I even tried to describe it to a salesperson helping me at the counter. I said it was fresh, light, citrusy, but not too much, and pleasant… not heavy or strong, just right.

She showed me a few colognes, but we didn't get anywhere. Then I asked if I could smell the Calvin Klein. Sure enough, that was it.

A flurry of memories came rushing back.

When my son was nine years old, he would sneak into our bathroom to help himself to his dad's cologne. He would spray the Calvin Klein on himself and go back and play in the yard, thinking I did not know what he had just done. Then he would come into the kitchen, where I would be preparing some meal or snack, and stand right next to me. I would look at him and smile, and he would sheepishly ask, "What, mom?" I wouldn't say anything to him except, "You smell good, son." Then we would both laugh.

He liked Calvin Klein. But since he did not live with me, and I didn't see him as much as I liked, I had completely forgotten that he was fond of that particular cologne.

I was very happy to have found the cologne. Moreover, I thought from then on it would function as a sign of my son's presence in my life.

September 22, 2006

On the suggestion of a coworker, I had bought a CD titled Many Lives, Many Masters, by psychotherapist Brian L. Weiss, MD. While listening to the disk, I realized that my son was communicating with me through the spoken words. The CD features a patient of Dr. Weiss who, under hypnosis, recalls past-life traumas that seem to hold the key to her recurring nightmares and anxiety attacks. She recalls her drowning in an 1863 flood, providing intricate details of her feelings in the moments before she drowns. Then, on Track 15, she talks about the fact that she has had 86 different lives. That's when I had goose bumps. At once I exited the freeway and pulled over to calm down, as my intuition was telling me this was how my son was communicating with me.

I was also conflicted to the extreme, as my rational self did its utmost to stand its ground. But then I would remember the following words of Nicola Tesla: "The day science begins to study non-physical phenomena, it will make more progress in one decade than in all the previous centuries of its existence."

I do believe that we are never alone, that we are part of a universe which has different names in different cultures and religions. To me, God is the universe, infinite and greater than the totality of the parts. When we expand our thinking, we start to comprehend it.

I believe the human mind is as yet incapable of seeing all of the various dimensions out there. Yet they do exist, as my son was to show me in my next dream.

Perhaps the time will come when all these things will be revealed, just like the fact that today 96% of the world is unseen to the human eye. In the meantime, I accept and appreciate the fact that my son communicates with me and brings back our shared memories — which otherwise I wouldn't be able to recall — through these phenomenal experiences.

Fourth experience

On May 25, 2007, my son visited me again and said, "Mom, I know you are still worried about me. I'm here to take you somewhere and you will see what a beautiful place I am at... I am sorry, but you will not be able to come inside. You will have to watch from a distance. Don't worry, I will be with you through the whole time as I show you where I am."

I was very curious to know where he was. Soon he took me to a bright light, a long, funnel- shaped space with magnificent colors. The light was extremely bright and pleasant to the eye, with lots of silver, pink, green, blue, light brown, and purple. There were also some soft colors. I had never seen anything like it.

I felt light, like a feather floating up. As the marvelous colors enveloped me, I could hear a soft, vibrating, and infinitely soothing tone. I couldn't see any part of my body. I didn't even feel like I had a body. I knew only that I was a being. I remember being mesmerized by the magical light. I was looking up and flying up. I could feel that other beings were around me. I couldn't tell who or what they were, but I could feel them vibrate.

My son showed me a large, bright-green and yellow butterfly with ovals on its wings. I could see through it. I had the distinct feeling that the butterfly and the other beings were made of light. These vibrating beings, detached from one another yet forming a glorious whole, were all part and parcel of the light and the magnificent colors which enfolded me. "Mom, do you feel the energy here?" my son asked. "And do you see what a beautiful place this is? I am with them all the time. They guide me everywhere. There is so much happiness here, and great things to learn, so many interesting things. I am showing you this because I don't want you to worry about me. I know that you are worried about me, but please don't be. Think of yourself, our family."

I said, "Yes. I feel it and I see it. It is a celestial place and I would stay with you here in this supremely good place."

"Now, mom, we have to stop," he said. "I can't take you any further from this point."

I said, "Please do. I want to see more of these dancing, vibrating lights."

He said, "No, mom. I love you a lot, but I can't let you go any further. I will take you back."

I felt there was no end to that funnel. The light was magnetic — so peaceful, calming, and full of wisdom. It felt as though I were in complete solitude, accepting fully who I was, among those beings. I felt I was a part of them and there was no one there who was going to judge me.

Each and every thing I experienced was in sync, positive, and moving cohesively around me. There was unity.

I wish I had that here on Earth: the unity of humans living together, with only a positive energy. It was a resplendent experience.

Fifth experience

One such occurrence happened on June 5, 2008. Carl was lying down on his gravesite, with only a towel on him. There was a light breeze. I walked over to him and said, "Son, you will catch a cold. Why don't you get up? Let's go inside." His response was, "Mom, it is so peaceful. I want to sleep here like this. Please leave me be."

I woke up to realize it was another dream. This time, however, unlike the aftermath of some previous dreams, I felt no panic. Only peace and calmness.

Sixth experience

On November 20, 2009, I fell asleep while watching a television program. I don't know how long I slept, but when I woke up, my son's presence was all around me. There were figure skaters on television, skating gracefully to "Appassionata," a piece by the Secret Garden ensemble. I had never heard it before. What I felt was reminiscent of the experience of being with my son in the funnel, with the vibrating energy enveloping me. Even though there was no enfolding light this time, I could still feel the energy around me. It was this very energy that had awakened me. I knew it was my son's energy. I was in tears. "I love you, son," I murmured. I knew he was there and I was very grateful for that moment.

My son's favorite number was 86. He was born in 1986, and the jersey he wore displayed the number 86. That jersey hangs in the Pickwick Ice Skating Center. Ever since my son's passing, that number has popped up frequently and everywhere: in stores, on license plates, on the back of a truck I was behind on the freeway once.

Then came December 6, 2013, when I rented a new apartment in a new city. As I called the utility company to set up automatic payments, the customer representative said an access code would be generated for me. "Your code, Miss, is 86-86."

I laughed and cried with gratitude. My son was letting me experience him once more. He let me know that even though I had moved, he was right there with me.

Thus my son has allowed me the freedom to live and experience each and every moment with him at my side.

Chapter six

Healing and the future

There is a saying in Tibetan, "Tragedy should be utilized as a source of strength." No matter what sorts of difficulties we face, how painful experience is, if we lose our hope, that's our real disaster.

Dalai Lama XIV

The messages I've received from my son have brought peace to my soul and helped me look at life differently. They have also given me the strength to write about my experiences and memories and publish them on a website and in this book.

I want every person devastated by the loss of a child or another loved one to know that it is entirely possible to regain one's moorings and go on to live a full life.

I have experienced, and continue to experience, the pain that you feel as you read this. After years of research in my quest to find answers to personal tragedy, I can tell you that that quest is simply never-ending. There is no answer as to why this happened to me or to my son. There is no answer as to why you are having to experience the pain, grief, and anger you are going through today. God did not do this to us, and it is no one's fault. Not yours, not anyone else's, and I want you not to blame yourself. It just happened. Who says the next five minutes are guaranteed to be safe for anyone? We hope that they are, but this is precisely where the disappointment stems from. It has to do with expectation: we naturally expect to have a long and healthy life. Yet the reality is that such a life is not guaranteed for anyone. We should instead open our minds and live life with love, compassion, and kindness towards everything and everyone, because that is how we are remembered and live on when we're gone.

In the process of coming to terms with the loss of my son, I learned to appreciate the special occasion called life. I learned to be grateful for each and every moment that we have on Earth, to do everything in our power to create happy memories with our loved ones, and, most importantly, to love abundantly.

Right now, as you look to the future, resolve to stop worrying about past misunderstandings or clashes with loved ones. Forgive and understand that we are not guaranteed a future; we are only promised the opportunity of today. Embrace life, learn to just be. Love, accept, allow yourself to discover the freedom of being thankful for the times you've had with those you miss. Create that which is positive and share that energy with those within your life's circle.

Through an ongoing string of otherworldly experiences, my son helped me look at life through a different lens, with greater clarity. I know within my heart that there is life after the physical body dies.

I hope you can relate to the experiences I've shared, and find a measure of comfort and solace by reading this book. Above all, I hope you can muster the courage, as I have, to share your experiences with others.

The purpose

Pain and suffering have come into your life, but remember pain, sorrow, suffering are but the kiss of Jesus — a sign that you have come so close to Him that He can kiss you.
Mother Teresa

For the past several years, I have often questioned myself as to what the purpose of my life should be following the loss of my son, in light of the extraordinary and ongoing experiences of feeling his presence around me and actually communicating with him through the medium of dream.

Was there a way of harnessing the power of those experiences to help others who struggled with grief? The question was all the more relevant since an increasing number of individuals seemed to want to discuss my loss and its aftermath. People, often complete strangers, would broach the subject by asking me how I was able to survive such a tragic loss, until, eventually, they would reveal to me that they, too, have just lost a child or another loved one. Many of them would also reveal that they blamed themselves for the loss and wonder if they could have prevented the death had they done something differently.

After contemplating for many years, I have decided to write this book to help grieving parents and individuals.

I know that you, too, are looking for answers, but finding none. When death comes at an older age, it is still difficult but we accept it, knowing it's a part of life's natural cycle. I think there is no end to the stages of grieving, no end to the process, when it comes to the death of your child, because we can never accept that it's a part of the natural cycle of life. If you are involved in an organization or group that can provide you with support, be open to it by all means. Furthermore, always feel free to contact me, as I am always eager to listen and share my story.

There is a higher power, an anchor, within us which can sustain us throughout the grieving process, as we struggle to identify a new purpose in our lives. It is by tapping into that universal power, not breaking away from it, that we're able to grow.

Everything in life is a process— a process to find your purpose. Sometimes, even if we think we've found our life's purpose, the loss of a loved one changes us in a way that nothing else can. The challenge then becomes to reconfigure our path, to learn to live with the deep scars of the spirit, and realign our purpose.

"The empty bedroom" of a departed love one will always be a part of our life. After all, we're only human, and our earthly life is fundamentally different than the eternal one, where our energy is surrounded with the light of love.

When I feel the emptiness within, I take out the suitcase of memories and let myself just be. It is only then that peace follows and I am able to go on to the next day.

Only people going through similar grief will understand the pain and suffering we experience. Certainly relatives, friends, and family members will be there for us for a while, and we should be grateful for that, but we will be carrying the pain of missing our child's physical presence for all time — just like my doctor had never stopped feeling the pain of his son's passing in the 30 years after his loss. That pain tends to visit us in waves, with seemingly interminable regularity.

When we receive communications from our lost loved one in various forms, they can help us take our days moment by moment and survive, so we can look forward and continue to live our lives. As we do this, we must remember that there is indeed an afterlife, and our loved one will be greeting us when it is our time to join them.

Thoughts from my heart

Do not judge the bereaved mother. She comes in many forms. She is breathing, but she is dying. She may look young, but inside she has become ancient. She smiles, but her heart sobs. She walks, she talks, she cooks, she cleans, she works, she is, but she is not, all at once. She is here, but part of her is elsewhere for eternity.

Unknown

Our emotions need to be as educated as our intellect. It is important to know how to feel, how to respond, and how to let life in so that it can touch you.

Jim Rohn

In 2007, I launched a website in my son's memory (virtual-memorials.com/main.php?action=view&mem_id=8630) in order to keep his spirit alive through the sharing of memories by his friends, loved ones, and myself.

The creation of the site took quite some time. Halfway through, however, I realized that the work was helping me heal. Expressing my feelings through poems, songs, and music enabled me to cope. I have written poetry ever since I was in ninth grade, so writing about how much I loved my son and the spectrum of experiences in connection with his loss as well as my healing process came naturally. Emanating from my heart, the words flowed onto paper, like a soothing, cleansing river.

The following are some of my poems, which are also posted on the website.

Ephemeral

On December sixth, nineteen eighty six,
God gave me my son as a very special gift,
To love, to cherish, and to protect him.
Who could have known?

With the first steps my son made in his attempt to walk,
I held his little hands very tight.
He wiggled but didn't fall.
In time, he walked very strong.
Then I had to learn how to let him go.
My little fellow walked on his own.

When it was time for him to ride his first bike,
I stood and watched him
So as prevent him from falling on his back.
Who could have known?

He was three years old when his sister was born.
My little son was there to help me around.
He played with her, held her very tight,
Made sure she didn't cry.
Who could have known?

In his first months in preschool he cried after me,
Slept on the bench in the school's library.
Back-to-school nights:
Math homework, learning the alphabet,
Mother and son talking.
He was very bright.
I read him stories every single night,
Stroking his back the way he liked,

Caressing his hair until he slept,
Then kissed his forehead, wished him good night.
Who could have known?

Hockey practices were next on our list.
Four days a week I carried his hockey sticks.
Occasionally he made me angry,
'Cause he played with his sister roughly.
He would rustle her and when she'd cry,
He'd say, "Sister, I'll give you everything,
But please don't cry…"
Who could have known?

An unfortunate divorce wiped out
The fun of the thirteen years.
The next six years were filled with thorns and bitterness.
My son stayed with his dad, chose not to see us.
His pockets were full of money at age thirteen,
Material things confused his thinking.
For years attempts to talk to him have failed.
One thing was left to do: ask for God's help.
I prayed that he'd be safe, take care of his health,
Until the day came and he'd understand.
But who could have known his life would be so brief,
And I'd be left behind drowning in my grief?

He turned nineteen in two thousand five,
Drowned in the lake while having fun.
God took back the gift once he had given me.
His purpose on this earth is complete.
Special memories he has left behind
Will be cherished for the rest of my life.
Who could have known I'd be left behind,
Drowning in my grief for the rest of my life?

Now I dance

I did not die, I did not die,
I simply passed from earth to sky.
From physical state to the unseen,
My energy vibrates and evolves.
I simply passed from earth to sky.
Now I dance with infinite stars.

Six months

It has been six months
You are not with us.
It is not easy,
Time goes by.

I miss you now
More than I ever did.
It is not easy,
Time goes by.

I visit your gravesite,
Placing nineteen white roses.
It is not easy,
Time goes by.

I hope when I speak
You can hear me.
It is not easy,
Time goes by.

I cry, think about good times,
Bad times, and everything in between.
It is not easy,
Time goes by.

A part of my future is empty now.
Thoughts of holding you in my arms again
Are over now.
It is not easy,
Time goes by.

The hope of one day
Meeting your girlfriend with you
Is over now.
It is not easy,
Time goes by.

Instead I met her without you, son.
She brought red roses and placed
Them on your grave.
It was not easy to watch that, my child.
Time goes by.

We hugged each other,
Cried in silence instead of smiling,
Both of us speechless.
I didn't know how to comfort her, my child.
Time goes by.

Unanswered questions,
Unspoken feelings
Left us in doubt,
My lovely child,
It is not easy,
Time goes by.

I hope we will be united,
This time in heaven.
Perhaps that time will be easier.
Time goes by.
Rest in peace, my child.

Further reading

Time Loops and Space Twists: How God Created the Universe, by Fred Alan Wolf.

The Yoga of Time Travel, by Fred Alan Wolf.

Hello from Heaven, by Bill Guggenheim and Judy Guggenheim.

Many Lives, Many Masters, by Brian L. Weiss.

Life After Life, by Raymond Moody and Elisabeth Kubler-Ross.

Reunions: Visionary Encounters with Departed Loved Ones, by Raymond Moody, Jr. and Paul Perry.

Walking in the Garden of Souls, by George Anderson and Andrew Barone.

Why Would a Good God Allow Suffering? by Kurt DerHaan.

How Can I live with my Loss? by Tim Jackson.

Why is Life so Unfair? Edited by Anne Cetas.

Is There Life After Death? by Elisabeth Kubler-Ross.

Ten Poems to Change your Life, by Roger Housden.

CPSIA information can be obtained
at www.ICGtesting.com
Printed in the USA
FSOW01n0648080816
23471FS

9 780996 772709